INNER REFLECTIONS

2002 Engagement Calendar

SELECTIONS FROM THE WRITINGS OF
PARAMAHANSA YOGANANDA

SELF-REALIZATION FELLOWSHIP

FRONT COVER:
Baltimore butterflies on Canada lilies, New York State
Photograph by Robert Lubeck / Animals Animals

NOTE: Holidays and other observed dates are included for the United States (U.S.), Canada,
the United Kingdom (U.K.), England (Eng.), Wales, Scotland (Scot.), Australia (Aus.), and New Zealand (N.Z.).

No part of this calendar may be reproduced in any form or by any means
without written permission from the publisher:
Self-Realization Fellowship, 3880 San Rafael Avenue, Los Angeles, California 90065-3298, U.S.A.

Printed by Graphicom, Italy
10676-17

THE SCENERY OF MOUNTAINS PAINTED ON THE EVER-CHANGING AZURE CAN-
VAS OF THE SKY, THE MYSTERIOUS MECHANISM OF THE HUMAN BODY, THE
ROSE, THE GREEN GRASS CARPET, THE MAGNANIMITY OF SOULS, THE LOFTI-
NESS OF MINDS, THE DEPTH OF LOVE—ALL THESE THINGS REMIND US OF A
GOD WHO IS BEAUTIFUL AND NOBLE.
                    —*Paramahansa Yogananda*

IN THIS CALENDAR we are happy to share with you some of the divine beauty that
reveals itself through the myriad forms of life and through our interaction with
the world around us. Whether spread over the vast heavens or hidden in the
exquisite delicacy of a tiny flower, that beauty is always beckoning, inviting us
to look behind the outward form and sense the presence of God within.

The photographs featured here are accompanied by selections from the
writings of Paramahansa Yogananda, whose timeless and universal teachings have
awakened many, of all races, cultures, and creeds, to a deeper awareness of the
One Reality that sustains and unites us all. We hope that the thoughts and
images in these pages will bring you inspiration and encouragement in the days
and weeks of the coming year.

Fall morning, Mt. Katahdin and Sandy Stream Pond, Baxter State Park, Maine
Photograph by Paul Rezendes

GOD IS ETERNAL LAUGHTER; A JOYFUL HEART IS HIS SMILE.

—*Paramahansa Yogananda*

Blue-eyed triplefin, New Zealand   *Photograph by Burt Jones and Maurine Shimlock*

OUR THOUGHTS ARE POWERFUL CREATIVE FORCES FLOATING IN THE ETHER
READY TO ACCOMPLISH THEIR PURPOSE....CONCENTRATION AND MEDITATION
TUNES THOSE THOUGHTS AND FOCUSES THEM ON MANIFESTING SUCCESS.

—Paramahansa Yogananda

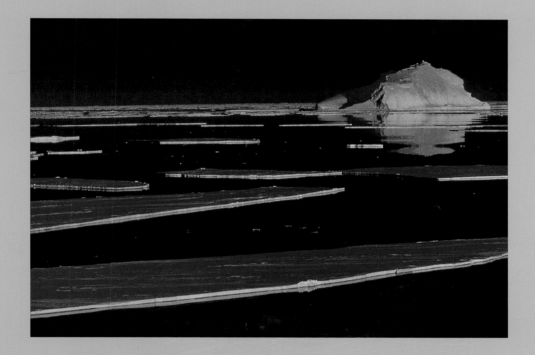

Icebergs, Antarctica   Photograph by Stefano Nicolini / Animals Animals

THE SOUL PERCEIVES IN ALL BEAUTY THE EXPRESSION OF DIVINE BEAUTY
AND FEELS A BLISSFUL EXPANSION OF CONSCIOUSNESS AND LOVE
THROUGH THAT EXPERIENCE.

—*Paramahansa Yogananda*

Peacock feather photographed on reflective surface   Photograph by Dick McMahon

TO WISH FOR PERFECTION FOR THE LOVED ONE, AND TO FEEL PURE JOY IN THINKING OF THAT SOUL, IS DIVINE LOVE.

—*Paramahansa Yogananda*

Fawn and mother in snowfall, Michigan   Photograph by Carl Sams

SPREAD THE FIRE OF SPIRIT THAT BURNS ALL DARKNESS FROM HUMAN LIVES.

—*Paramahansa Yogananda*

Lava from Kilauea volcano entering ocean, Volcanoes National Park, Hawaii
Photograph by G. Brad Lewis

JUST AS THE TREE IS HIDDEN IN THE SMALL SEED, SO IS THE
DIVINE KNOWLEDGE OF OMNIPRESENCE HIDDEN IN THE SOUL.
—*Paramahansa Yogananda*

Paca leaf seedpod in rain forest, Amazonas, Brazil   Photograph by Carlos A. Sastoque

LOVE IS THE DIVINE POWER OF ATTRACTION IN CREATION
THAT HARMONIZES, UNITES, BINDS TOGETHER.

—*Paramahansa Yogananda*

Greater flamingos, Ngorongoro Conservation Area, Tanzania   Photograph by Kirk Yarnell / SuperStock

EVERY SYMBOL IN NATURE IS A MATERIALIZATION OF THE RAYS OF
GOD....ALTHOUGH WE ARE DIFFERENT IN APPEARANCE, WE ARE ALL SYMBOLS
OF THE INFINITE, OF THAT VAST FORCE OF GOD.

—*Paramahansa Yogananda*

Cup coral, Red Sea   Photograph by Jeff Rotman

MATTER APPEARS AS A VISIBLE, TANGIBLE FORM,
BUT IN REALITY IT IS COMPOSED OF UNSEEN ELECTROMAGNETIC WAVES....
THESE WAVES ARE "FROZEN" LIGHT.
—*Paramahansa Yogananda*

Ice on beach, The Netherlands   Photograph by Jan-Peter Lahall

PERFORM ALL DUTIES SERENELY, SATURATED WITH PEACE. BEHIND THE THROB OF YOUR HEART, YOU SHALL FEEL THE THROB OF GOD'S PEACE.

—*Paramahansa Yogananda*

Great white egrets in morning mist, Switzerland   Photograph by Andrea Bonetti

LIFE AND DEATH ARE BUT DIFFERENT PHASES OF BEING.
YOU ARE A PART OF THE ETERNAL LIFE.

—*Paramahansa Yogananda*

Hepatica flowers, Michigan   Photograph by Loretta Williams

NO ONE ELSE HAS A PERSONALITY JUST LIKE YOURS. NO ONE ELSE HAS A FACE LIKE YOURS. NO ONE ELSE HAS A SOUL LIKE YOURS. YOU ARE A UNIQUE CREATION OF GOD.

—*Paramahansa Yogananda*

Common sea dragon, Jervis Bay, Australia   Photograph by Fred Bavendam / Minden Pictures

YOU SHOULD LOOK AT LIFE UNMASKED, IN THE MIRROR OF YOUR
EXPERIENCES....LOOK AT THE PERPETUAL CURRENT OF EMOTIONS AND
THOUGHTS THAT ARISE WITHIN YOU....SEEK UNDERSTANDING WITH YOUR
HIGHEST INTELLIGENCE, WISDOM, LOVE, AND VISION.

—*Paramahansa Yogananda*

Great blue heron after sunset, Ding Darling National Wildlife Reserve, Florida
Photograph by Charles Sleicher / Stone

JUST AS A PERSON HAS DREAMS THAT SEEM REAL FOR A TIME BUT LOSE THEIR
VALIDITY WHEN HE EMERGES INTO THE WAKING STATE OF CONSCIOUSNESS,
SO IT IS POSSIBLE FOR MAN TO AWAKEN FROM THE DREAM OF MATTER-REALITY
AND TO LIVE IN THE CHANGELESS REALM OF SPIRIT.

—*Paramahansa Yogananda*

Canyon reflections in stream, Death Hollow, Utah   Photograph by Jack Dykinga

YOU CAN MAKE PERMANENT HAPPINESS FOR YOURSELF BY NOT LETTING
ANYTHING EVER DISTURB YOU ON YOUR FORWARD JOURNEY TO SUCCESS.

—*Paramahansa Yogananda*

Western box turtle, Texas   Photograph by Tim Fitzharris / Minden Pictures

IN THE DEEPER STATE OF CALMNESS, ONE PERCEIVES IN THAT STILLNESS
THE MOONÈD REFLECTION OF GOD'S PRESENCE.

—*Paramahansa Yogananda*

Moonrise over Kenai Mountains and Homer Spit, Alaska   Photograph by John Pezzenti

CONSIDER NO ONE A STRANGER.
LEARN TO FEEL THAT EVERYBODY IS AKIN TO YOU.

—*Paramahansa Yogananda*

White-tailed fawn and pine squirrel, Montana   Photograph by Alan Nelson / Animals Animals

EVERYTHING IN THE LORD'S CREATION HAS SOME SPECIFIC UTILITY.
ALL MATTER, HOWEVER INSIGNIFICANT, HAS A
PARTICULAR PURPOSE AND EFFECT.

—*Paramahansa Yogananda*

Ladybug on toadstool, Veluwe Nature Reserve, The Netherlands   *Photograph by Jan Vermeer*

IN NATURE YOU BEHOLD THE MOTHER ASPECT OF GOD, FULL OF BEAUTY,
GENTLENESS, TENDERNESS, AND KINDNESS.

—*Paramahansa Yogananda*

Lioness carrying cub, Masai-Mara, Kenya   Photograph by Michel Denis-Huot

THE SOUL ATTUNED WITH GOD IS DEEPLY SENSITIVE TO BEAUTY
IN ALL FORMS, AND SEEKS EVER TO EXPRESS BEAUTY
IN THE LITTLE AS WELL AS THE BIG DETAILS OF LIVING.

—*Paramahansa Yogananda*

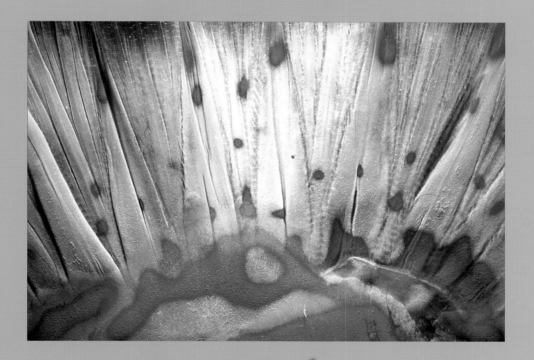

Tail of parrot fish, Red Sea   Photograph by Jeff Rotman

YOU ARE IMMORTAL AND ARE ENDOWED WITH ETERNAL JOY. NEVER FORGET THIS DURING YOUR PLAY WITH CHANGEABLE MORTAL LIFE.

—*Paramahansa Yogananda*

Great egret displaying, Venice Rookery, Florida   Photograph by Arthur Morris

WE SHOULD BATHE OUR SPIRITS IN THE DEEP, PURE FEELING THAT STIRS
WITHIN US WHEN WE GAZE ON THE GLORIES OF HIS CREATION.
THIS IS THE WAY TO KNOW GOD AS BEAUTY.

—*Paramahansa Yogananda*

Mandarin fish, Lembeth Strait, Indonesia   Photograph by Constantinos Petrinos

HUMBLY SERVING ALL WITH THEIR BEAUTY, FLOWERS SAY MORE TO US ABOUT GOD THAN ANYTHING ELSE. EACH ONE BRINGS A MESSAGE THAT THE HEAVENLY FATHER IS RIGHT HERE.

—*Paramahansa Yogananda*

Lady slipper orchids, Oulanka National Park, Finland   Photograph by Paavo Hamunen

YOUR FATHER LOVES YOU UNCONDITIONALLY....IT DOESN'T MATTER HOW
MANY MISTAKES YOU HAVE MADE; THEY ARE ONLY TEMPORARY.

—*Paramahansa Yogananda*

Male lion with cub, Masai-Mara, Kenya
Photograph by Anup Shah / BBC Natural History Unit Picture Library

YOU SHOULD ALWAYS BE SPARKLING *WITHIN* WITH INFINITE WIT AND LIGHT.

—*Paramahansa Yogananda*

Flowers reflecting in dewdrops, Oregon   Photograph by Steve Terrill

MASSIVE UNIVERSES AND THEIR TINIEST PARTICLES, MAJESTIC GODS OF NATURE
AND THE MOST INSIGNIFICANT OF CREATURES...ALL HOLD THEIR SPECIAL
PLACE IN THE CONFORMATION OF THE COSMIC IMAGE.

—*Paramahansa Yogananda*

Blue darner dragonfly, Santa Fe, New Mexico   Photograph by Tim Fitzharris

LIMITATION AND DEFEAT MUST NEVER BE ACCEPTED....THE TRULY ADMIRABLE
ARE THOSE WHO TRANSMUTE ADVERSITY INTO A PERSONAL VICTORY.

—*Paramahansa Yogananda*

Silhouette of horse rearing, western Oregon   *Photograph by Ron Kimball*

DO NOT BE SATISFIED WITH DROPS OF WISDOM FROM SCANTY EARTHLY
SOURCES; RATHER, SEEK WISDOM WITHOUT MEASURE FROM GOD'S
ALL-POSSESSING, ALL-BOUNTIFUL HANDS.

—*Paramahansa Yogananda*

Bleeding hearts above pool, Bellingham, Washington   *Photograph by Steve Satushek / Image Bank*

TO GET AWAY FROM EVERYTHING NOW AND THEN GIVES A PERSON A
CHANCE TO THINK WHAT LIFE IS ALL ABOUT.
—*Paramahansa Yogananda*

Llama overlooking Machu Picchu, Peru   Photograph by Frans Lanting / Minden Pictures

TRANQUILITY IS THE NATURE OF GOD.

—*Paramahansa Yogananda*

Redwood trees and rhododendrons, California   Photograph by Ron Sanford

TRUST MORE IN GOD. BELIEVE THAT HE WHO
CREATED YOU WILL MAINTAIN YOU.

—*Paramahansa Yogananda*

Lowland gorilla and baby, Wild Animal Park, Kent, England   Photograph by Art Wolfe

BE AS SIMPLE AS YOU CAN BE; YOU WILL BE ASTONISHED TO SEE HOW
UNCOMPLICATED AND HAPPY YOUR LIFE CAN BECOME.

—*Paramahansa Yogananda*

Boisduval's Blue butterfly on horsetail, Nutrioso, Arizona   Photograph by Beth Kingsley Hawkins

PURITY, PEACE, HAPPINESS BEYOND DREAMS, ARE SPARKLING AND
DANCING WITHIN YOUR SOUL.
—*Paramahansa Yogananda*

Dwarf birch in autumn tundra, Denali National Park, Alaska
Photograph by John Eastcott and Yva Momatiuk

TO LIVE IN THE INNER, BOUNDLESS SOUL-PEACE...IS REAL PARADISE.
WHETHER IN A PALACE OR UNDER A TREE,
WE MUST CARRY WITH US ALWAYS THIS INNER HEAVEN.

—*Paramahansa Yogananda*

Cherry tree and mute swan, Victoria, British Columbia   Photograph by Michael Orton / Stone

IF YOU HAVE A CLEAR UNDERSTANDING, THEN NO MATTER WHAT CLOUDS OTHERS TRY TO CREATE, YOU WILL SEE WHAT IS RIGHT.

—*Paramahansa Yogananda*

Storm at sunset, Etosha National Park, Namibia   Photograph by Claudia du Plessis

KEEP A SECRET CHAMBER OF SILENCE WITHIN YOURSELF, WHERE YOU WILL
NOT LET MOODS, TRIALS, BATTLES, OR INHARMONY ENTER....
IN THIS CHAMBER OF PEACE, GOD WILL VISIT YOU.

—*Paramahansa Yogananda*

Octopus inside shell, Lembeth Strait, Indonesia   Photograph by Constantinos Petrinos

BE A LIVING TREE, CONSTANTLY SPREADING OUT NEW GROWTH.
THE STRONG-HEARTED SOUL SAYS, "THERE IS SUNSHINE
IN MY LIFE, AND I HAVE EVERY CHANCE TO THROW OUT
SHOOTS AND BRANCHES OF ACCOMPLISHMENT."

—*Paramahansa Yogananda*

Red laceleaf Japanese maple tree, The Japanese Garden, Portland, Oregon   *Photograph by Jon Gnass*

YOU ARE A CHILD OF GOD. YOU HAVE ALL THE POWER NECESSARY
TO TAKE YOURSELF WHERE YOU WANT TO GO.

—*Paramahansa Yogananda*

Spotted bush cricket leaping, Cambridge, England
Photograph by John Brackenbury / Woodfall Wild Images

QUIET PLACES ARE NATURALLY CONDUCIVE TO INNER CALMNESS, BUT IF YOU
ARE DETERMINED, YOU CAN REMAIN INWARDLY UNDISTURBED
REGARDLESS OF ANY COMMOTION AROUND YOU.

—*Paramahansa Yogananda*

Pika in clouds near Paradise, Mt. Rainier National Park, Washington   Photograph by Jamie Wild

ALL KINDS OF SEEDS OF POWER ARE WITHIN YOU,
WAITING FOR YOU TO DEVELOP THEM.

—*Paramahansa Yogananda*

Milkweed seeds in autumn, Pennsylvania   Photograph by Nancy Rotenberg / Animals Animals

COME INTO THE SILENCE OF SOLITUDE, AND THE VIBRATION THERE WILL
TALK TO YOU THROUGH THE VOICE OF GOD.

—*Paramahansa Yogananda*

Harvard Pond Wetlands at dawn, Petersham, Massachusetts   Photograph by Paul Rezendes

HARMONIZE YOUR THOUGHTS AND DESIRES WITH THE ALL-FULFILLING
REALITIES YOU ALREADY POSSESS IN YOUR SOUL. THEN YOU WILL SEE
THE UNDERLYING HARMONY IN YOUR LIFE AND IN ALL NATURE.

—*Paramahansa Yogananda*

Black-headed gulls, Bath, England   Photograph by Raoul Slater / Woodfall Wild Images

GOD IS...NOT ONLY THE VIBRATING ENERGY AND CONSCIOUSNESS THAT
PERVADE EVERYTHING, BUT ALSO THE "FROZEN" ENERGY AND
CONSCIOUSNESS THAT WE BEHOLD AS MATTER.

—*Paramahansa Yogananda*

Water drops on rushes, North Cascades National Park, Washington   Photograph by John Dittli

WE ARE IMMORTAL SOULS, DESTINED TO RETURN ONE DAY
TO OUR HOME IN GOD.
—*Paramahansa Yogananda*

Canada geese and rising moon, Manitoba, Canada   *Photograph by Scott Nielsen*

FEEL PEACE ALL AROUND YOU....
FEEL THE PEACEFUL GLOW OF THE FATHER WITHIN.

—*Paramahansa Yogananda*

Caribbean reef squid at night, Cayman Islands   Photograph by Mike Kelly

ARISE FROM DREAMS OF LIMITING MORTAL BOUNDARIES TO THE REALIZATION
OF THE VASTNESS OF THE IMMORTAL SOUL WITHIN YOU.

—*Paramahansa Yogananda*

Mountains in evening fog, Geneva, Switzerland   Photograph by Peter Baumann / Animals Animals

GRATEFUL FRIENDS ARE ONLY THE LORD IN DISGUISE,
LOOKING AFTER HIS OWN.

—*Paramahansa Yogananda*

Chestnut-mandibled toucans, Colombia, South America   Photograph by Art Wolfe

As soon as the sun of wisdom comes, it gives a smile that lifts from the heart the delusive cloud of despondency and bathes the garden of the soul in the light of faith and power.

—*Paramahansa Yogananda*

Flowers backlit by sun, Härna, Sweden   Photograph by Jan Töve Johansson

MAINTAIN YOUR EQUILIBRIUM AMIDST TRYING CIRCUMSTANCES....
STAND UNSHAKEN BY ADVERSE TURNS OF EVENTS.
—*Paramahansa Yogananda*

Opossum, South Lyon, Michigan   Photograph by Steve Gettle

WE SHOULD TRAIN OURSELVES TO THINK IN GRAND TERMS:
ETERNITY! INFINITY!

—*Paramahansa Yogananda*

Land, water, and trees, Alberta, Canada   Photograph by Jan-Peter Lahall

WITH CALCULATED PRECISION GOD HAS ORDAINED THE
STRUCTURAL FORM OF EACH LIVING THING.

—*Paramahansa Yogananda*

Fall leaves, Great Smoky Mountains National Park, North Carolina
Photograph by Stephen Kirkpatrick

WITH THE DAWN OF DIVINE EXPERIENCE, WITH THE DAWN OF DIVINE JOY,
WE BEHOLD THE GLIMMER OF BEAUTIFUL THOUGHTS AND
EXPERIENCES WITHIN OUR HEART.

—*Paramahansa Yogananda*

Water lilies, Okavango Delta, Botswana   Photograph by Frans Lanting / Minden Pictures

WITH UNFLINCHING STEADINESS MARCH ON YOUR PATH, BELIEVING THAT THE INFINITE CREATIVE POWER IS BEHIND YOU.

—Paramahansa Yogananda

Gemsbok on Namib Desert, Namibia   Photograph by Theo Allofs

December

s	m	t	w	t	f	s
	1	2	3	4	5	6	7
8	9	10	11	12	13	14
15	16	17	18	19	20	21
22	23	24	25	26	27	28
29	30	31				

December/January

30
monday

31
tuesday

1
wednesday

New Year's Day

2
thursday

New Moon ●   *Bank Holiday (Scot.)*

3
friday

4
saturday

5
sunday

Paramahansa Yogananda's Birthday

January 2003

s	m	t	w	t	f	s
				1	2	3	4
5	6	7	8	9	10	11
12	13	14	15	16	17	18
19	20	21	22	23	24	25
26	27	28	29	30	31	

ACKNOWLEDGMENTS

～

We wish to express our sincere appreciation to the following photographers and agencies who contributed to this year's *Inner Reflections* engagement calendar. Following a contributor's name in parentheses is the month and first day of the week, or other description, where each photo appears.

Theo Allofs (12/30)

Animals Animals
(cover; 1/7; 4/22; 9/30; 11/11)

Peter Baumann (11/11)

Fred Bavendam (3/18)

BBC Natural History Picture Unit
(6/10)

Andrea Bonetti (3/4)

John Brackenbury (9/16)

Michel Denis-Huot (5/6)

John Dittli (10/21)

Claudia du Plessis (8/26)

Jack Dykinga (4/1)

John Eastcott / Yva Momatiuk (8/12)

Tim Fitzharris (4/8; 6/24)

Steve Gettle (12/2)

Jon Gnass (9/9)

Paavo Hamunen (6/3)

Beth Kingsley Hawkins (8/5)

Image Bank (7/8)

Jan Töve Johansson (11/25)

Burt Jones / Maurine Shimlock (1/1)

Mike Kelly (11/4)

Ron Kimball (7/1)

Stephen Kirkpatrick (12/16)

Jan-Peter Lahall (2/25; 12/9)

Frans Lanting (7/15; 12/23)

G. Brad Lewis (1/28)

Robert Lubeck (cover)

Dick McMahon (1/21)

Minden Pictures
(3/18; 4/8; 7/15; 12/23)

Arthur Morris (5/20)

Alan Nelson (4/22)

Stefano Nicolini (1/14)

Scott Nielsen (10/28)

Michael Orton (8/19)

Constantinos Petrinos (5/27; 9/2)

John Pezzenti (4/15)

Paul Rezendes (opening photo; 10/7)

Nancy Rotenberg (9/30)

Jeff Rotman (2/18; 5/13)

Carl Sams (1/21)

Ron Sanford (7/22)

Carlos A. Sastoque (2/4)

Steve Satushek (7/8)

Anup Shah (6/10)

Raoul Slater (10/14)

Charles Sleicher (3/25)

Stone (3/25; 8/19)

SuperStock (2/11)

Steve Terrill (6/17)

Jan Vermeer (4/29)

Jamie Wild (9/23)

Loretta Williams (3/11)

Art Wolfe (7/29; 11/18)

Woodfall Wild Images (9/16; 10/14)

Kirk Yarnell (2/11)

"THE IDEAL OF LOVE FOR GOD AND SERVICE TO HUMANITY FOUND FULL EXPRESSION IN THE LIFE OF PARAMAHANSA YOGANANDA....THOUGH THE MAJOR PART OF HIS LIFE WAS SPENT OUTSIDE INDIA, STILL HE TAKES HIS PLACE AMONG OUR GREAT SAINTS. HIS WORK CONTINUES TO GROW AND SHINE EVER MORE BRIGHTLY, DRAWING PEOPLE EVERYWHERE ON THE PATH OF THE PILGRIMAGE OF THE SPIRIT."

—from a tribute by the Government of India upon issuing a special commemorative stamp in honor of

PARAMAHANSA YOGANANDA
1893–1952

BORN IN NORTHERN INDIA IN 1893, Paramahansa Yogananda came to the United States in 1920 as a delegate to an international congress of religious leaders convening in Boston. He remained in the West for the better part of the next thirty-two years, until his passing in 1952. Reporting at that time on his life and work, a Los Angeles periodical wrote: "Yogananda made an outstanding cultural and spiritual contribution in furthering the cause of better understanding between East and West. He combined in a conspicuous degree the spiritual idealism of India with practical activity of the West....The centers he established, the great numbers he inspired to nobler living, and the ideals he planted in the common consciousness of humanity will ever remain a monument to his notable achievement."

Self-Realization Fellowship, the international nonprofit society founded by Paramahansa Yogananda in 1920, is dedicated to carrying on his spiritual and humanitarian work — fostering a spirit of greater harmony and understanding among those of all nations and faiths, and introducing to truth-seekers all over the world his universal teachings on the ancient science of Yoga.

Paramahansa Yogananda's life story, *Autobiography of a Yogi*, is considered a modern spiritual classic. It has been translated into eighteen languages and is widely used in college and university courses. A perennial best-seller since it was first published more than fifty years ago, the book has found its way into the hearts of readers around the world.

An introductory booklet about the life and teachings of Paramahansa Yogananda and a book catalog are available upon request.

SELF-REALIZATION FELLOWSHIP
3880 San Rafael Avenue • Los Angeles, California 90065-3298
Telephone (323) 225-2471 • Fax (323) 225-5088
http://www.yogananda-srf.org

IMPORTANT NUMBERS

NAME

ADDRESS

CITY

STATE AND ZIP

PHONE   FAX

E-MAIL

NAME

ADDRESS

CITY

STATE AND ZIP

PHONE   FAX

E-MAIL

NAME

ADDRESS

CITY

STATE AND ZIP

PHONE   FAX

E-MAIL

NAME

ADDRESS

CITY

STATE AND ZIP

PHONE   FAX

E-MAIL

NOTES

NOTES